Simple Wire Sculpture

Frontispiece Cobra. Wire and string.

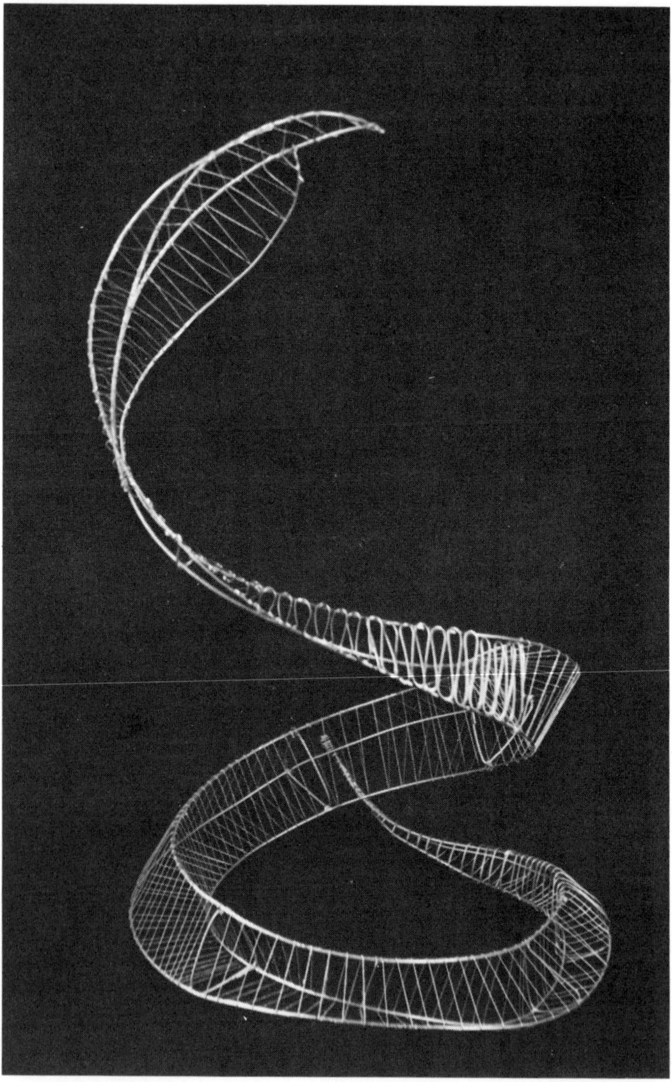

Simple wire sculpture

Elizabeth Gallop

Studio Vista

Acknowledgements

The author would like to make the following acknowledgements for illustrations and examples of wire sculpture used in this book: to the staff and students of Salisbury College of Art for figs 15, 32, 51a, 52, 54, 55, 56a, c and d, 60, 66, 74; to J. Waldron Esq. and the University of Keele, Staffordshire for fig. 2; to A. H. Trost Esq. for fig. 25 (photograph); to the Galerie Daniel Gervis, Paris, for fig. 42; to the Trustees of the British Museum for figs 43 and 44; to the Albert Loeg and Krugier Gallery, New York for fig. 50; to Miss H. Ainsey for fig. 53 (sculpture); to W. A. Chaplin Esq. for fig. 66 (photograph); to A. H. Richardson Esq. for fig. 70 (sculpture); and would like to thank D. Perry, R. Gallop, and N. and J. Gallop for their assistance, and J. Barker Esq. of Salisbury College of Art for his guidance and encouragement.
All the wire work, photographs and drawings not mentioned here were done by the author.

General Editors Janey O'Riordan and Brenda Herbert
© Elizabeth Gallop 1970
Reprinted 1974
Published in Great Britain by Studio Vista
Cassell and Collier Macmillan Publishers Limited
35 Red Lion Square, London WC1R 4SG
Set in 9 on 9½ pt Univers 689
Printed and bound in the Netherlands
by Grafische Industrie Haarlem B.V.
ISBN 0 289 79679 2

Contents

Introduction

Since the very beginning of art, man has used lines as a means of representing the things he sees about him, either purely for decoration or as symbols with a definite meaning and purpose. Wire sculpture is really an extension of line drawing; an endlessly exciting way of drawing in space.

Many people need a little encouragement to extend their practical experience in drawing and painting to that of sculpture, where the problems appear much greater. Apart from the difficulties of working in three dimensions, the lack of a work-shop or facilities for carving and modelling may deter some would-be sculptors.

Wire sculpture establishes a link between drawing and sculpture. The complete beginner can get accustomed to handling a solid material by using it at first for 'drawing' flat designs, graduating to relief work and then to compositions in the round. Designing in wire is a very good introduction to sculpture and helps the beginner to think in three dimensions, to pick out the essentials in an object or idea, and to think in terms of the areas *not* filled in, as well as the solid shapes which are familiar in traditional carving. Those who are already proficient in other forms of sculpture will find in wire work fresh methods of expression and unaccustomed relationships of line and space. Working with a new medium, one begins to see things in a different way; an unusual view of the commonplace is often very stimulating. Constructions using a modern material such as wire have only recently been accepted and understood as art, and so the field is open to all kinds of developments and new ideas.

The craft of bending and soldering wire can be used in many practical ways, and once the small amount of equipment is assembled you will find that many things you would like to make for your home are now within your scope. Quite a wide selection of articles are described in this book, but I am sure you will find plenty more either useful or purely decorative items which will fit in with your individual interests.

Objects in wire cannot be on a very large scale and for this reason it is a good material for the amateur working at home. There is very little mess and the materials are inexpensive and easily obtained, they do not have to be bought from a specialist dealer. Once you have mastered the simple technique and have fully understood the limitations of the material, all your attention can be concentrated on the design; there are limitations to all materials

Fig 2 *The Tragapogan* by Jack Waldron. Large stainless steel construction. *Keele University*

7

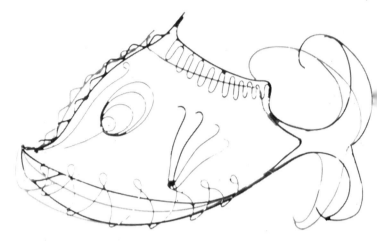

Fig 3 Fish. Galvanized wire

and it is important not to ignore them; they give a framework on which to base a design, so that the material and the work you do with it have a sympathy of feeling between them. It is hard to point out exactly why a piece of work looks uncomfortable and strained, but often the reason is that the material has been used against its inclination.

Although the methods and ideas I have described will give you plenty of material to work on, and it will be helpful for you to see how a particular wire construction has been built up, I would like to stress that a distinctive individual style depends on developing your own means of putting ideas into wire. So, as long as your wire work stays together, allow the excitement of creating to carry you on from one idea to another.

I hope you will feel as much enthusiasm as I do for this modern type of sculpture which can produce such lively and often amusing results.

1   Materials and tools

The few tools needed for working with wire are to be found in most homes, while some extra equipment can be made from everyday objects. As in all craft activities, there are additional tools and more expensive materials which give excellent results, but it is best to begin with the very simplest and then increase the number as you gain experience.

Wire

GALVANIZED WIRE
Inexpensive, and can be bought in any hardware shop. It can be shaped, soldered or glued, and painted without any difficulty, and so is very useful both for experimenting and for making all kinds of household articles and permanent sculpture. Wire is usually sold by weight in various thicknesses, the gauge being the same as that of knitting needles: 20g is fine and only suitable for small objects or for use together with heavier wire, while 12g – roughly the size of a matchstick – cannot be bent smoothly by hand and is used for strong simple frameworks, or nearly straight sections of wire. 16g and 18g are the most adaptable, being stiff enough to retain their shape but not too resistant to bending.

BRASS AND COPPER WIRE
Obtainable in grades ranging from hard to soft. The medium and soft are particularly good for decorative craft-work, especially where no solder or glue is employed; the wire is very easy to work, and may be lacquered to keep the polish. The thicker gauges can be fashioned much more easily than the thicker galvanized wire and very professional-looking things can be made. The thinner brass and copper wire makes attractive contemporary jewelry. However, it is not usually very easy to buy this type of wire, and it is considerably more expensive than galvanized.

SILVER WIRE
Still more costly, and is generally only employed for jewelry or very delicate work.

PICTURE WIRE
Brass or copper, made of fine twisted strands; although it is very thin it has a lustre which has great attraction in costume jewelry and miniature toy making.

FINE FUSE WIRE
Used to bind and strengthen glued joints or to add contrast to sculptures made of strong wire.

PLASTIC COATED ELECTRIC WIRE
Very pliable, and children find its gay colours fun to use.

Materials for joining wire

The simplest way of joining wire is to twist one piece onto another, but in many cases this is not sufficiently rigid and the joints have to be fastened more firmly.

PLASTIC STICKY TAPE
Generally sold as insulating tape or as framing for pictures. The variety of colours make it possible to match plastic coated wire to give almost invisible joints, and the sticky backing adheres well when a rough-textured tape is bound tightly round on itself. This method is applicable to any kind of wire for small-scale work.

EPOXY RESIN GLUE
The modern resin glues form quite a strong bond with metal, and they are a great help in wire craft, but there are disadvantages which must be taken into account when making a three-dimensional object. The resin is mixed with a hardener and takes several hours to set, the time being reduced by heating. This means that each join has to be held immobile during this period, and the job progresses rather slowly. Work which can be laid out and held in place as a whole, such as a flat picture, or anything made of continuous lengths of wire with only a few final joins,

Fig 4   Joins. **a** twisted **b** taped **c** soldered **d** glued

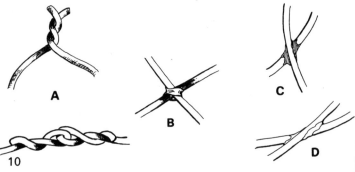

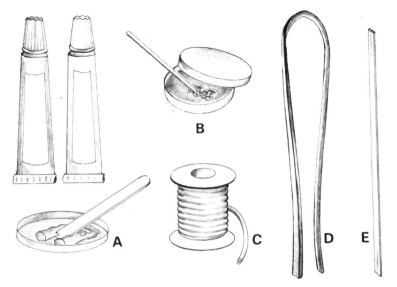

Fig 5 Materials.
a epoxy glue: resin and hardener b solder paste c cored solder d blowpipe solder e silver solder

would be good subjects for gluing. But if a lot of unions are necessary, in positions that are awkward to support, it will be found more convenient to use solder, which sets instantly and can be re-melted for alterations. The techniques of soldering and gluing are described in chapter 3.

Solder

There are various types of solder, and it is worth experimenting to find the one which suits you best and which proves most satisfactory for the work you wish to do. There are hard and soft solders, and as the names suggest, they melt at different temperatures and result in stronger or softer joints.

SOFT SOLDERS

These can be obtained in a number of forms. There are very low melting point alloys which melt below the temperature of boiling water, and others which melt in the heat of a meths (alcohol) flame or a candle. Some solders, developed primarily for electrical work, combine flux and solder; these are easy to use on the very fine wires. An example is solder paint – finely divided solder suspended in flux – which is painted onto the wire and then heated while the parts are gripped together. Also cored solder, a thin tube of solder with flux in the centre, which puts flux and solder on the joint in one operation as the heat is applied.

11

Soft solder melting between 170°C (370°F) and 260°C (564°F) is fast to work with and holds strongly on any gauge of wire. It is used in conjunction with a suitable flux (see below) and requires a blowpipe or gas torch. You will find after some practice that it is very satisfactory for large open constructions, for heavy wire, and for work which is likely to be handled frequently. The most convenient type for wire work is blowpipe solder sold in 2 oz. strips about $\frac{1}{4}$ in. thick.

HARD SOLDER
Hard solder consists of silver, alloyed with other metals in differing proportions depending on the characteristics required. Although more expensive than soft solder, it is economical to use, and with a gas torch, or blowpipe for small items, the results are very clean and strong.

Flux

When soldering it is necessary for the coating of the wire to be free from dirt, grease and oxides. A rub with emery paper will clean the metal, but flux is essential to prevent oxides forming and to give the solder a bite onto the wire. There are proprietary (commercial) makes of flux suitable for any soldering requirements.

FLUX FOR SOFT SOLDER
It is better to use a ready-made brand of flux if one is available, but killed spirit can be made at home in the following way: pure concentrated hydrochloric acid is placed in a ceramic or glass pot, preferably out of doors, and small pieces of sheet zinc are dropped in, the reaction being allowed to die down after adding each piece, until there is undissolved zinc left in the jar. As this resulting liquid is corrosive and poisonous it is advisable to use a low heavy jar which cannot easily be knocked over, and the material should be stored safely.

Flux can be bought in paste form and applied with a long splinter of wood, and as a liquid which can be spread on the wire with a feather.

FLUX FOR HARD SOLDER
Borax, made into a paste with water, is the traditional flux for hard solder, but there are versatile fluxes which can be purchased for use with any silver solder, and the wire craftsman will find them very helpful.

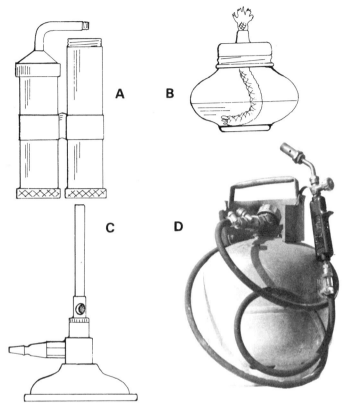

Fig 6   Heating equipment.
   a automatic spirit·(alcohol) blowpipe **b** simple meths (alcohol) burner
   c bunsen burner **d** gas cylinder and torch

Heating equipment

Certain points should be considered before selecting your means of heating. Wire sculpture is a matter of building up, and it is almost impossible to assemble every piece in place and do all the soldering at once, unless the work is simple or can be laid out flat. Therefore it is best to have a flame that can be left burning economically or can easily be relit. A smoky flame will deposit soot and prevent the solder from uniting with the wire. It is undesirable to have an upright heater such as a meths (alcohol) flame or bunsen burner without a blowpipe, as the molten solder will drop onto it and stop it functioning properly.

The burner must generate enough heat to melt quickly and efficiently the particular solder you are using.

Fig. 7 Stand. Metal rack on bricks with (l. to r.) pliers, weight, gas torch, solder, clothes peg (clothespin), flux, water and brush

BLOWPIPES

Pressure is necessary to make an upright flame sharp and hot, and directed at an angle towards the work.

If a fine blowpipe is held in the mouth and a light continuous stream of air is directed across a bunsen or meths (alcohol) burner, a thin hot flame results. This is simple and very efficient for small-scale jobs. The automatic blowpipe in fig. 6 burns meths (alcohol), and builds up its own pressure giving a sharp, fierce flame.

ELECTRIC SOLDERING IRON

Many people have a soldering iron designed for electrical work, which can be used with multicore solder on thin wire, but on the thicker gauges the heat is dissipated too fast for the proper soldering heat to be achieved. Also, since the iron must actually be held in contact with the wire a tricky join can easily be displaced.

GAS TORCH

Since picnic gas cylinders are now so universally used, the addition of a soldering torch attachment is not too costly. For safety always connect the torch and cylinder by high pressure tubing. The gas torch is so adaptable and economical for all kinds of solder and wire that I must recommend it as the most suitable means of heating for any wire work you may wish to do.

14

Stand

For most soldering it is better to place three-dimensional work on the open mesh of a stand, rather than directly on a fireproof surface where the heat is spread unnecessarily and the solder is inclined to collect in ugly lumps on the underside of the work. An old cake-cooling stand or any firm metal mesh placed on bricks is perfectly adequate. Your work can then be clamped onto the bars to keep it still, with the flame directed from underneath if necessary, and none of the heat is wasted. A tray below will catch any excess solder, which can be re-used, and a piece of smaller mesh placed on the rack will prevent delicate work falling between the bars.

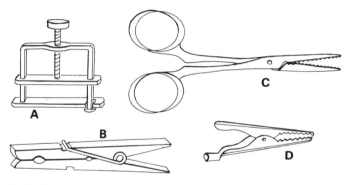

Fig 8   For holding joins.
a screw clip b wooden clothes peg (clothespin) c surgeon's clamp
d electrical clip

Clips and weights

When wire is either glued or soldered it is essential to keep the joints in firm contact until setting is complete. Any small heavy metal objects or stones can be used to keep flat wire arrangements in place. The problems are greatly increased when a three-dimensional construction is being built up. Weights will help to hold it firmly at the base and bricks are useful to prop up different sections, but when attaching one wire to another where they cannot be supported, then keeping them in good contact is more difficult. There are various screw and spring clips to be bought in either tool shops or electrical suppliers, and surgeon's clamps and screw clips can also be effective.

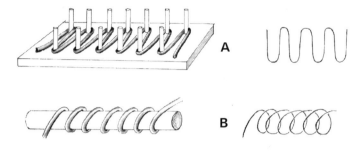

Fig 9   Jigs.
a for continuous bends b for long spirals

Metal clips will get very hot and tend to conduct the heat away from the joint when soldering, but they are good for holding the wires closely for gluing. A fastener that needs to be unscrewed can put a strain on the unfinished work as it is moved from one joint to another, and a heavy clamp may pull the work out of place by weight or leverage.

Wooden spring clothes pegs (clothespins) have more advantages than any of the more conventional clips. They are light, do not get hot, and can be moved quickly; they can be shaped for any job, such as a joint involving two very different thicknesses of wire. Of course they cannot be put in the direct path of a flame, but it is usually quite easy to avoid setting fire to them. They are inexpensive to replace and can be bought anywhere.

Plasticine or clay

These materials are very useful for temporary holding, or to keep several joints in place while an unsatisfactory part is altered. Also a lump of plasticine on the bench is a help when designing a sculpture, as it can be used to hold wires in various experimental positions before making a joint.

Jig

For a series of similar shapes of wire, a jig can be made with thin dowel in a board, suitably spaced. For long spirals, have a collection of different sizes of dowel, straight and tapered.

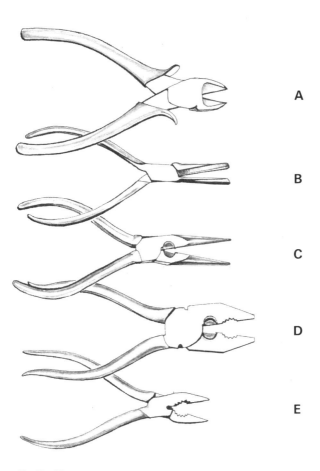

Fig 10 Pliers.
a diagonal cutters b duck bill c snipe nose d household e small

Pliers and wire cutters

For the simplest work using soft or plastic covered wire, only a pair of household pliers are needed, as most of the work can be done with the fingers. But for the harder wires it is a help to have at least two pairs of pliers, and additional specially-shaped tools make bending and shaping easier. Round nosed, flat ended, and very small pliers, and piano-wire cutters all help to simplify the work. For very heavy wire a small hacksaw should be used. A vice is helpful when bending short, strong wires.

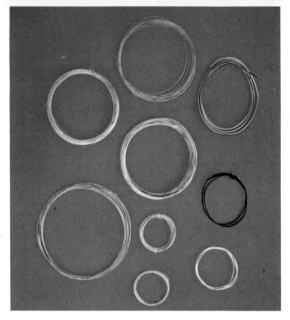

Fig 11   Wire.
From top to bottom (left) 20g galvanized, 12g galvanized; (centre) 18g copper, 12g brass, brass and copper picture wire; (right) electric wire: twin cable, single wire from a cable, twin bell wire.

Fig 12   Flower holder

2   Wire shaping

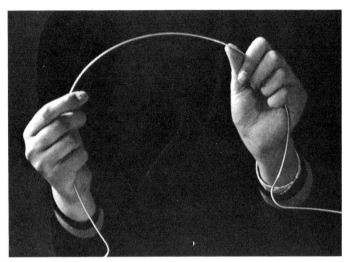

Fig 13   Curving wire

CURVES

The final effect of any wire work, whether ornamental or practical, can be impaired if each wire is not shaped really smoothly.
If you try to alter the curve of wire by a series of jerks using the
hands close together, the result is usually angular and unsatisfactory. To form a curve or simple curl, grip one end of the wire in
pliers and, holding the wire with the other hand at least a foot
away, swing it round quite slowly and smoothly, trying to utilize
the original curve of the coiled wire rather than fighting against
it. For the final shaping, stroke along the wire between fingers
and thumb, easing it into the exact curve you need. When you have
experience of the way wire behaves you can make any type of
simple or complex curve by drawing it strongly but evenly over the
ball of the thumb. Be ready to use only a small part of a curve,
select just one section with exactly the right characteristics.

SPIRALS

For a tight flat spiral, hold the very tip of the wire in fine pliers
and wind slowly round as for curves but forming into a flat disc
as the circles increase in size. Stop to shape the wire carefully
if the curve is not even, as corrections are more difficult when
the spiral is complete. Another method is to form a little loop
at the end of the wire, hold this flat in the pliers and work the

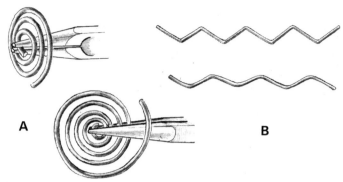

Fig 14   Wire shaping.
a making spiral discs b wiggles

Fig 15   (*opposite*)   Sea horse, using continuous wires with very few joins

wire round, sliding the progressively coiling wire through the pliers, gripping the centre while actually bending; a large disc can be continued outside the jaws when it gets too big (fig. 14a).

These discs can be pulled down from the centre to make a cone, or the same shape obtained by winding the wire round a tapering object. Where more movement and life is wanted, irregular spirals, or discs wound with the centre pressed to one side, look very effective.

SPRINGS
Springs are formed round a suitable stick, wound regularly and then either compressed or extended to give any variation needed.

STRAIGHTS
As wire usually comes in coils, it is often a problem to make perfectly straight pieces. By slow, even stroking between finger and thumb against the curve, the wire can be gradually straightened. Don't try to remove all the curve in the first attempt; make successive strokes, avoiding kinks.

WIGGLES
Where a straight line would look too harsh, a wavy line might fit in better. Use wide pliers to get an equally spaced angular wave, or use fingers or round pliers for a softer effect.

SHARP ANGLES
These can be made by gripping the wire in pliers or in a vice and bending tightly over a sharp corner, or by bending the wire further than the angle needed and bringing it back to the right position. Hairpin bends are hard to make in the thick gauges because the compression on the inside and the stretch on the

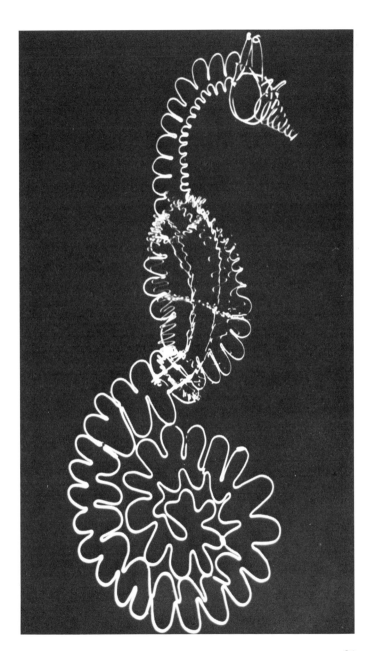

outside are too great for the metal, but by bending as far as possible and then squeezing in the vice, a fairly good result is obtained.

Continuous designs

BATTLEMENT DESIGN

Hold one end of a long wire in the left hand and, working continuously towards the right, bend downwards over the ball of the right thumb and up again round the top of the forefinger. With practice a rhythm of movement is acquired, giving very even bending.

Variations (fig. 16a)
a   graded down in size
b   pulled out into a zigzag
c   pulled round in a flat circle
d   bent into a collar
e   each bend opened to a right angle in alternate directions
f   two lengths superimposed on each other

ARABESQUE

This is more difficult to do, and should be practised on thin wire until a fairly uniform pattern can be produced. It is a very adaptable filler and gives a good illusion of solidity.

With the length of wire vertical, hold the lower end in the left hand, and starting two inches up the wire, bend it down over the right thumb using the fingers to swing it round into a loop, always making the natural curve work with you. Change hands and make a loop in the opposite direction, taking the wire in front of each loop so that the finished arabesque lies evenly.

Variations (fig. 16b)
a   pull out to make the loops smaller
b   grade down in size
c   press together to make a very close design
d   make into a flat circle of four or more sections
e   form into a collar
f   make a shoulder under each loop
Although a series of round pegs on a board can be used as a jig for repetitive work, mechanical evenness is not as lively as the slight variations produced by hand, and it is worth persevering until you can make designs without this assistance.

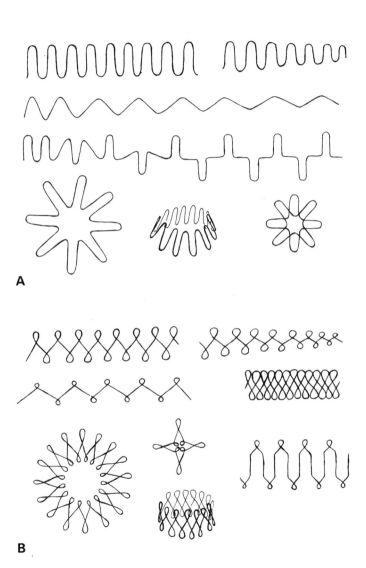

A

B

Fig 16   Continuous designs

23

3 Solder and glue: technique

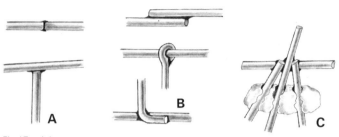

Fig 17 Joints.
a weak **b** strong **c** multiple joints firmly held for soldering

Both solder and glue only hold to the coating of the wire and so the joints are not infallible. It is important both to master the technique of soldering and gluing and to design in such a way that the least possible strain is put on the joint. By following a few guiding suggestions, a great many of the troubles of construction can be sidestepped and the disappointment of making a delightful sculpture which gradually falls apart can be avoided.

Designing for strength

For each project, choose wire which has the necessary strength to support the weight of the finished piece and which will give the design a definite enough outline to catch the eye, at the same time being sufficiently workable to shape smoothly. A large and complicated structure made of very thin material is inclined to look flimsy and weak, while very thick wire will kink rather than curve and the results are untidy. Combining different gauges will give point to the design, and help to make it rigid without heaviness.

Strong joints can only be achieved if the wires are held undisturbed until setting is complete and if there is a good area of contact between the parts. The weakest bond will be in butt-joints: that is, when the cut ends are attached directly to each other. Although this may seem neat, it is never worth attempting; the area is so small that it seldom holds for long, particularly in a framework. The ends should be overlapped and may be filed smooth if a very tidy joint is required. T-junctions also should be given a larger area of attachment by bending one wire at right angles to lie against the back of its companion, or by making a loop at the end of one piece to fit round the other (fig. 17). If the appearance of a very delicate part of the design would be spoilt by a strengthened T-junction, then see that each section has a strong surround of wire or has a line running behind it to prevent twisting on the weak joins.

Where several wires cross together or the joints are very close to one another, hold them temporarily with plasticine or clay until you are sure where every wire has to fit, and then attach them all at once. Keep the plasticine near, but not on, the place to be glued or soldered, as the oil in it will interfere with the adhesion (fig. 17). Alternatively, use a hard solder for the first joins and a low melting-point solder for subsequent joins; or you can use solder followed by glue so that there is no chance of detaching parts already in place.

If a large framework is being made or wires are projected away from the main body, then care should be taken to give them adequate support. The leverage and bend on a long wire pulls on the joints and as much judicious strengthening as possible is needed. Doubling up the main lines and filling corners will help, without spoiling the original design with too many props and fillers. When bending the wire into shape it is advisable to see that it maintains the position you want without tension. If you force it into place and clamp without shaping carefully, the joint is very likely to spring apart.

To reduce the number of joins, each one of which is a point of weakness, it is advisable to organize your ideas and, instead of using a lot of short wires, use continuous designs from long wires to give the same, and often better, results. Try to see the finished pattern you want for a section, and draw it. Imagine that you cannot take the pencil off the paper, and devise an unbroken design which can be translated into wire (see fig. 15, page 21).

Individual pieces of sculpture call for individual treatment and one should not fall back too often on the same ideas, but the two basic patterns and their variations on pages 22–3 can be used in many ways.

Prefabricate as much as you can. Once you have decided on the effect you want, do a lot of the intricate work separately and add the whole section to the main frame with as little soldering as possible. It makes the work neater to assemble and encourages you to plan ahead. If a prefabricated part seems unsatisfactory it can be abandoned without upsetting the main structure.

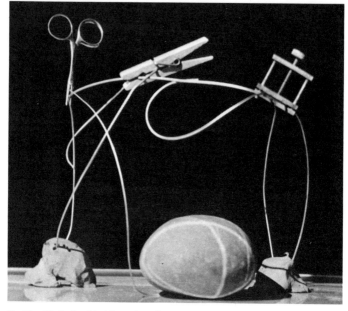

Fig 18   Methods of holding: clay, clamp, peg (clothespin), weight, screw clip

Any object made in wire is likely to be picked up by one strand, and with the amount of play there is in wire all the joints will be subject to strain; therefore the construction must be stronger than might seem necessary.

Holding

One of the problems when constructing any wire work is to hold the components in exactly the right place while soldering or gluing. When making a flat object, the pieces can be laid over the rack and held by weights for soldering, or on paper over a smooth surface for gluing, and as long as the intersections are in really close contact there are few difficulties. But when building up a three-dimensional sculpture it is often very hard to keep each piece in its place. Try to make a stiff frame, to give something solid to work from, even if it is only one part of the sculpture. It is preferable to construct the whole outline, or guidelines, and add double wires where extra toughness seems desirable. To ensure firm contact and accurate alignment of the wires, use any method of holding, or a combination of several, such as pegs (clothespins), clay, clips, clamps, or solid supports (see page 15).

26

Gluing

The epoxy resin glues will only bond properly if the surface of the wire is absolutely free from grease or dirt, so the cleaning process is vital if a lasting joint is to be accomplished. Rub the parts to be joined with emery paper to roughen and clean them, then wash well in detergent to remove all grease, rinse in warm water and dry without fingering again.

The maker's directions for mixing hardener and resin should be followed; a filler is sometimes advised for mixing with the glue to make application easier. For particular types of work the manufacturers will give advice on the best formula of glue to use. The resin sets very much faster if it can be heated and this makes the building up of sections of wire work less tedious. The setting times vary from 24 hours at 20 °C (68 °F), to 20 minutes at 100 °C (212 °F). Clamp the pieces so that they will not move during setting, but not so tightly that the glue is squeezed out completely from the touching surfaces, and then lay the work over a radiator or in a very low oven.

Mix only enough of the resin and hardener for the immediate gluing you have prepared; the results will be disappointing if semi-set glue is used.

Soldering—soft solder

Try soldering odd bits of wire before embarking on a full-scale piece of work. You have to get to know the characteristics of your own soldering torch and the type of solder and flux you have chosen to use. If the solder fails to hold, the wire has to be re-cleaned before a successful joint is possible—so make mistakes you can throw away.

To ensure a good joint, rub the wires shiny with emery paper and clamp them together. Smear or brush a little flux (page 12) onto the intersection. The flux helps the solder to run right into the joint. If you are using a small burner and blowpipe which gives a very localized point of heat, keep the end of the blowpipe just above the wick or mouth of the burner and just touching the flame, and blow gently and, as far as possible, continuously. With a gas torch, adjust to a sharp blue flame so that the heat can be applied to one spot without spreading to joints already set. The direction of the flame has to be watched, as one is inclined to overlook the fact that it is directed at a joint on the far side of the work which will probably melt and spring apart.

Holding the stick of solder in one hand and the torch in the other, just warm the solder without melting it, then direct the flame at the wire for a few seconds; you will see the flux running over the metal and the coating of the wire appears to go cloudy. Touch the wire with the solder only long enough for a bead of it to run into the joint, and then withdraw it from the flame. Continue to heat the joint until the solder combines cleanly with the coating of the wire.

A soldered joint should be perfectly smooth without any ugly lumps sticking to it. If the heat of the wire is insufficient the solder collects in blobs without really holding, while overheating causes it to roll straight off and then the joint must be cooled, cleaned, and re-fluxed before the solder will take.

Remember that molten solder runs downhill, therefore arrange the work so that the solder will run downwards into the joint, rather than trying to apply it from the side or below. If two different thicknesses of wire are to be joined, the thick one will require a little preliminary heating, otherwise the heavy wire will not be hot enough to take the solder or the thin one will become too hot.

Immediately after soldering each joint the excess flux is washed off, using a pot of water and a thick artist's brush, to prevent it discolouring and corroding the wire. This also makes the solder set quickly and the wire is then cool enough to handle.

Finally, when the whole article is finished, brush carefully in warm water and detergent, rinse and dry.

Silver soldering

Silver or hard solder has to be heated to a higher temperature than soft solder but the resulting join is stronger. To prepare a silver solder flux, moisten a lump of borax and rub this on a slightly rough surface to make a paste. The metal to be joined should be scraped very clean, and the stick of solder and the wire then smeared with borax paste or with a ready-made silver solder flux. Using a gas torch, heat the wire and solder slowly at first to melt the borax, and then to a dull red heat when the solder will run into the joint. Cool slowly, do not quench immediately with cold water. Finally wash well in plenty of water.

If a framework is completed with silver solder, then soft solder can be employed for the details without the danger of the main joints coming undone.

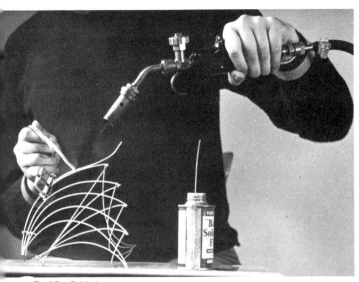

Fig 19   Soldering.
         a using a gas torch **b** cooling the soldered joint

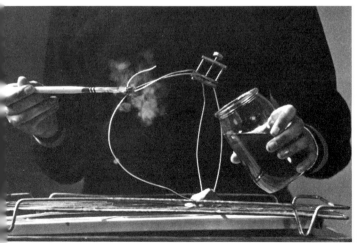

4   Wire work without solder

Fig 20   Deer and dachshund. Electric wire, slotted

Many charming articles can be made without the necessity of soldering. Soft brass wire, copper wire, picture wire and plastic coated electric wire need only simple methods of joining. Depending on the size and use to which it will be put, the object can be shaped without any means of holding together, or the wire may be twisted onto itself. Binding the joins with plastic sticky tape or using epoxy resin glue extends the range to flat sculpture or three-dimensional constructions with a small proportion of joints which are not likely to be subjected to too much strain.

The limitations of these simple methods soon become obvious when more ambitious and complicated structures are attempted, and in these cases solder is far more satisfactory.

Plastic coated electric wire

Colourful plastic wires, round or flat, provide possibilities for gay and amusing decorations. There should be a strong enough core in the wire to retain the shape you want; some electric wire is too springy for the purpose. Twin bell-wire or the divided parts of household cable, each one with a core of several wires, are easily worked and joined. Take advantage of the wide choice of colours available to add to the cheerfulness of your decorations.

JOINING
Fig. 21 shows several ways of making use of the inner wires at junctions. The bell wire with two separate wires is split to

30

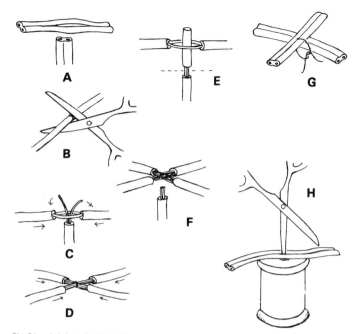

Fig 21   Joining electric wire.
  a slotting **b** ringing with scissors, the sleeve then slipped back or cut away
  c, d, e, f various methods of joining with inner wire **g** sewing **h** making
  a slit

allow another piece to be slipped through (a). The deer in fig. 20 is
easily made this way and needs no other means of holding. Cable,
with a bunch of inner wires, is joined by various methods as shown
in fig. 21 (c–f). The plastic coating is cut in a ring with scissors
which are not sharp enough to break the inner wires (b), and
sometimes the sleeve can be slipped back, and the join made and
then tightened by pushing the sleeve over it again. When a slit
is required in the wire, place it over the hole in a cotton reel (spool
of thread), and press the sharp point of scissors through until the
split is the correct size (h).

Sticky tape or strips of plastic coated shelf covering can be
used to bind the junctions, but some wire is very slippery and the
tape will only stay on if it is a rough textured one which will
stick firmly onto itself.

The wires can be sewn together (fig. 21g), using a strong needle
and button thread of the right colour. Pliers are usually needed to
push the needle through.

Fig 22   Names and badge, using electric wire

NAMES

Names made from plastic wire look almost like wrought iron when carefully done, they can be attached to doors or boxes, or to painted boards for hanging up. Flat wire set on edge makes the lettering stand out well without being too clumsy to bend round corners. Draw a good clear style of letter and bend the wire to fit; in some words a continuous length can be used, but it will look muddled if the lines fold back on themselves. When the letters are made singly, overlap the joins, shave them flat, and tape or sew them together. Make an interesting underline and fix the letters on this. An impact glue or plastic cement used for model-making will glue the letters onto a surface. These will not stand up to very hard wear so choose a fairly static position.

BADGES

Following the same method, make badges for school or club, scouts and guides, using suitably coloured wire stuck on painted boards. Draw the full-size badge on squared or graph paper to be sure it is symmetrical and correctly proportioned. If any bends are too sharp for the thickness of the plastic, cut a nick in the under-side to allow the sides to lie closer together. These badges are

Fig 23 *Moonscape*. Electric wire sculpture by 12-year-olds

useful to hang on a door or wall or could be made as a trophy or award.

SCULPTURES

There is no need to be tied down to conventional styles of sculpture, try any sort of bundling and looping until something interesting develops; working with such pliable wire will help to free your ideas. Coil the wire into different springs and join up as amusing animals and figures, make use of the double wire or the inner wires to increase the scope of your work. Try making brightly coloured primitive masks, either quite flat or with raised features but without anything at the back to confuse the appearance.

Brass and copper wire

Brass and copper wire in the medium and soft range is very readily shaped compared with similar thicknesses of galvanized wire. Lacquer will prevent the finished article from tarnishing.

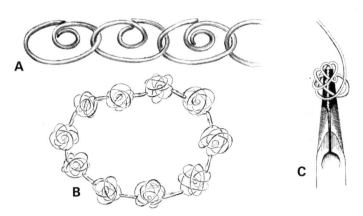

Fig 24   Using brass and copper wire.
    a belt links, 12g brass wire **b** bracelet, 22g copper wire **c** making a wire ball

JEWELRY

Although jewelry making is a specialized subject, a few rather modern and attractive things can be made using copper wire without the need of any means of joining, unless a little resin glue is employed to prevent the pieces being pulled apart by mistake.

Necklace or bracelet in copper wire (fig. 24b). Take 8 in. lengths of 22g soft copper wire, run the wire firmly over the ball of the thumb to smooth it out. Then, holding the very tip of the length in fine pliers, wind the wire loosely round in all directions, stopping to ease the curls into smooth circles until you have a little ball about ½ in. in diameter. Tuck the sharp end into the middle. Cut ¾ in. pieces of copper wire, bend up the ends like a staple, and hook the balls together, pressing the link ends down neatly.. Shorter lengths are used for smaller balls, grading down in size for the sides of the necklace. Finish with lacquer to keep the polished surface.

Experiment with flat links and other simple shapes to make chain belts (fig. 24a) or single pieces as pendants or ear-rings. Where these articles may come apart, a spot of resin glue will help to make them more lasting; follow the instructions for cleaning and gluing in chapter 3.

WALL DECORATION

A contemporary wall decoration is easily made using 16g brass or copper wire and plastic adhesive tape. Galvanized wire is difficult to manage in a large panel of continuous lengths as it is often troublesome to make it lie flat. Take long pieces and bend at right angles into squares and oblongs of different sizes and shapes, binding with thin strips of tape where the wires cross, and

Fig 25   Giraffe

Fig 26   Starfish. Galvanized wire, glued

weaving under when necessary to keep the whole panel as flat as possible. Get as great a variety of interest as you can in the way you arrange the lines, and then glue the whole piece onto a painted board. For a more colourful effect, mark some of the squares before gluing and paint them in bright colours to accentuate some parts of the design.

Galvanized wire

THE STARFISH

Fig. 26 is made with 18g galvanized wire, and glued. The finished decoration is quite strong and looks pleasant painted silver and hung on a dark wall. Draw out the five pointed design, varying the size and curve of each limb to make the starfish lively.

Shape the outer line from one length of wire, a 50 in. length is needed for a diameter of about 15 in. For the inner lines, form similar shapes, exaggerating the shape and gradually reducing the size, and arranging the joins to come at different places. Lay them inside each other with the lines touching on one side of each limb, until the unfilled centre is about 3 in. across. Coil an asymmetric centre to fit the space. Carefully rub the touching wires with emery paper, wash in detergent, rinse and dry without fingering these areas again, and lay the pieces of the starfish out on a sheet of paper. Spread a film of resin glue on each surface

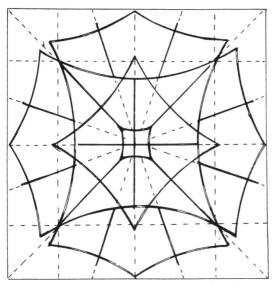

Fig 27 Guidelines on paper for the design in fig. 28, with main wires laid out for gluing

to be glued and use weights or light clamps, away from the glue, to keep everything in place. If you have an oven or radiator, heat the sculpture to 100°C (212°F), to speed up the setting. When hard, peel off the paper gently and the starfish is ready for painting (see page 47). If you find it difficult to keep all the bits in place, stick a few at a time, allowing the glue to set before adding the next batch.

SYMMETRICAL DESIGN

For a symmetrical decoration radiating from the centre, as opposed to a freely abstract design, it is essential to have all the angles and measurements similar in each segment, however many are chosen, so that a perfectly even result is obtained. The segments are either exactly similar or they can be in couples as mirror images of each other.

After you have sketched some possibilities, and decided on one you like, take a piece of paper as large as the final decoration and, starting from the middle, draw accurate guidelines to mark the segments, and also the centre of each one. The design can be drawn completely on squared or graph paper, and every wire fitted onto its place, or using the guidelines it can be built up as the fancy takes you, repeating each line section by section. Do not expect too much of the glue, outlying parts in particular must have a good area for the glue to hold.

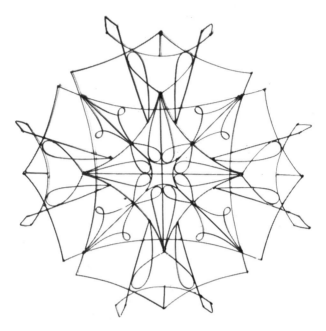

Fig 28   Symmetrical design in 18g galvanized wire

Lay the main frame of wires on the paper first, and then glue. If the work is to be heated, place small weights round the design to hold the paper flat, otherwise the heat will cause it to curl up and displace the wires. Some wires must cross, and the work will be stronger if they do, so arrange them to lie most easily over or under each other, propping up temporarily with cardboard or short pieces of wire to be sure of close contact for the glue. When this framework is set add the intermediate shapes, gluing and heating in stages until the design is finished. The paper can then be peeled off carefully and the piece is ready for painting.

The design in fig. 28 is 18 in. across, using 18g wire. It could be mounted on a contrasting board by gluing or by wiring as described for the lobster panel on page 46. It could also be framed in a circle of wire, gluing at the eight outer points, and hung directly on a wall.

TEAPOT STAND
To make a teapot stand using resin adhesive, take a cork mat or suitably cut piece of wood and some 16g and 18g galvanized

Fig 29 Teapot stand. 16g galvanized wire glued onto a cork mat

wire. To prevent the wire sticking to the mat before finishing, and to keep a check on where each wire should go, first place a piece of paper on the mat, cut to the same size. Bend a length of 16g wire to make a border, not quite at the edge, and attach this firmly to the mat with pegs (clothespins); then lay out your design, by eye as far as you can – a little irregularity lends character to anything which does not set out to be absolutely symmetrical – using the 18g wire. In this case none of the lines must cross or the surface of the mat will be uneven. Divide the design into four segments, cutting and shaping the wire to fit accurately, and fill each with a related but different shape. Draw round your wire onto the paper so that you know where every piece is to go, and assemble the main lines only, gluing the joints and clamping or weighting to keep them in place. Add the rest of the lines when the first glue is set. Finally, remove the paper, paint the design with a heat-resistant paint, and glue to the mat, pressing well to give good contact for the adhesive.

Sets of table mats can be made in this way, although they will not stand very hot oven dishes. Small drink mats (coasters) are attractive using a close design in thin wire.

5 Simple constructions using solder

Flat objects present fewest problems for the beginner in soldering. The frame for a climbing indoor plant is a good example, as it must be sturdy enough to support the plant but it can be made flat which simplifies the technique of soldering. From here we can progress to more complex three-dimensional objects where solder is advantageous because of the instant setting and the firm bond it makes with the wire.

Making a plant support

Climbing indoor plants need a support, and with wire you can make something more ornamental than the usual sticks or knitting needles. When deciding on the thickness of wire to use, the appearance, purpose and required strength of the article must be taken into account. A large open-work construction needs the heaviest workable wire to keep it rigid and to make it sufficiently visible.

To make the stand illustrated in fig. 30, take about 4 ft. of 16g galvanized wire and form the outer frame (a); this will make a support about 18 in. high. Bend the two inner frames (b and c) and lay all three together, cut the centre rib, hook over at both ends and pinch firmly, clamping or weighting all the pieces in place on the soldering stand and making sure that the cross-over lies neatly. Following the instructions for soft soldering in chapter 3, solder the junctions, taking care that all the wires are included where there are more than two at any point. It will probably be necessary to turn the work over to solder the back where the seven wires cross. Lay this framework on paper and draw the shape of the centre section; then draw the zigzags for each side of the middle rib, not necessarily exactly similar but with the points meeting on the centre line. Bend lengths of wire to correspond with these zigzag lines, arrange on the stand for soldering, weighting or clamping them onto the bars, and solder the inner points down the centre line. The outer edges of the zigzags can then be attached wherever they touch the inner frame; it is not easy to make all the bends quite accurate, so some angles may have to be missed. Wash the frame well to remove any residue of flux and give two coats of paint (see page 47) to prevent it rusting in the soil.

Fig. 31 shows another frame in use. A formal pattern or a free abstract design would also be attractive.

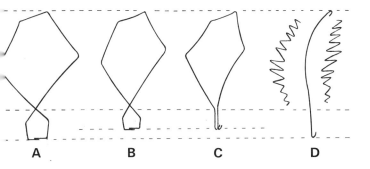

A   B   C   D

Fig 30   Parts of the plant support. **a** outer wire **b, c** inner frames **d** centre rib and zigzags **e** completed support

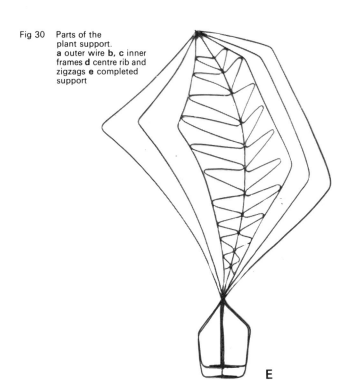

E

41

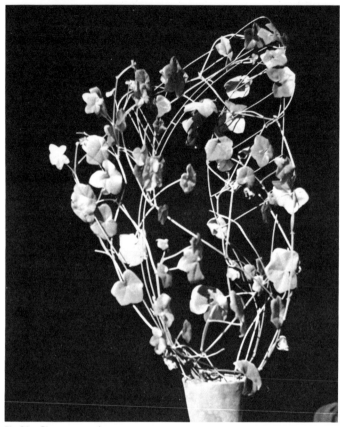

Fig 31   Plant support in use

Fig 32 (*opposite*)   Fish. Galvanized wire, soldered

Natural forms

Children like making outlines of their favourite animals and
these ideas can be extended to more sophisticated designs for
use as decorations. Flying birds, butterflies and insects look
modern and pleasing without the over-pretty appearance of some
similar ornaments made in other materials.

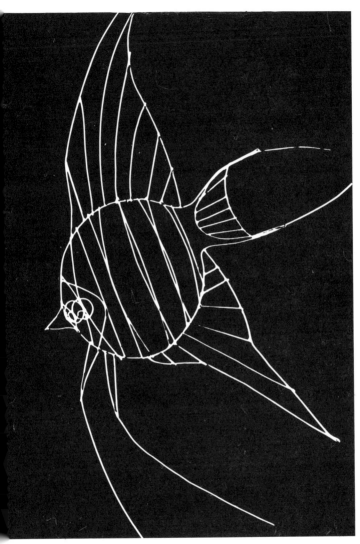

If a fish, bird, or insect is to be undertaken, try to find something unusual. After sketching your first idea, vary it, add to what you see, exaggerate, put in some movement, and look at the spaces you are creating as well as the lines, watching the relationship of one line to another. Remember to keep the joins as few as possible.

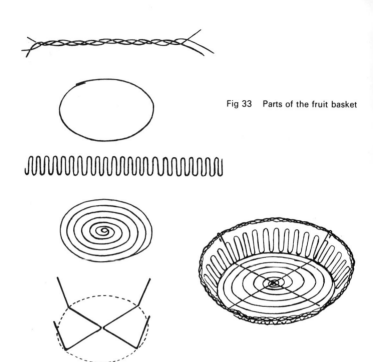

Fig 33   Parts of the fruit basket

Fruit basket

Use either brass or galvanized wire, 18g. The parts are shown in fig. 33. Coil the bottom as evenly as possible, lay over the two strengtheners and solder at every point. Make the continuous design for the sides, stand this in place and solder first to the strengtheners and then at each point round the bottom coil. Solder a circle of wire, adjusting the shape round a suitably sized plate or bowl, and slip it inside the four uprights. The edge is made simply by plaiting (braiding) three wires together, each wire must be bent slightly throughout the plaiting to keep it tight enough to look tidy. The plait is slipped onto the uprights and rests on the circle of wire. The uprights are then bent over, and the basket is completed with a few spots of solder to keep the edging in place.

Fig 34   Fruit basket in use

Pictures in wire

We have seen that glue or tape can be used successfully to put together fairly simple decorative panels, either attached to a board or hung on a wall, but when making a more complicated flat decoration, which perhaps will have to be cleaned frequently, or an abstract panel which you want to build up as you go along without drawing carefully beforehand, you will find soldering easier and more permanent.

Most houses have a wall which looks empty, and yet is not suitable for a framed picture – the high wall of the stairs, an awkward wall in the hall, or in the bathroom. Decide what type of wire work would look best – representational or abstract, very open or rather dense – and gradually an idea will emerge for just the right wall decoration. It could be quite a formal design, even picking up the design in the carpet or curtains. It could be a theme using people, buildings, machines or just shapes.

45

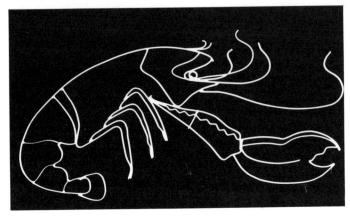

Fig 35   Lobster door panel

THE LOBSTER

Fig. 35 was made to hang on a larder (pantry) door, with similar panels on other cupboard doors as a guide to their contents, brightening up the kitchen in an unusual way. The whole lobster was soldered together first and then two very small holes bored through the door under the strongest wires. A thin hairpin of wire could then be slipped over the design and through the hole, and bent over at the back, holding it firmly but allowing easy removal and replacement for cleaning.

REPETITIVE PANELS

Another way of filling a wall space is to choose a unit, in itself an interesting shape, and repeat it to make as large a panel as you need. The spaces between the repeated units thus become an important factor in the total design. Make sure the shapes touch and can be soldered together at several points to make the panel strong enough for its size. A final framing of wire helps to give it a finish and also adds to its strength (see fig. 94).

These panels, either pictorial or abstract, may be used as fire-screens by attaching them to a painted panel, or a plastic-coated board such as that used for work surfaces and tables, as a background.

HOUSE NAMES AND NUMBERS

Continuing the idea of wire names suggested on page 32, use soldered wire to outline a painted house name or number; this

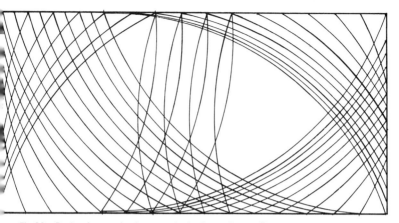

Fig 36   Design for panel using curved wire from a large roll

helps to make it stand out clearly, especially if a strong wire is used and doubled to give an effect of shadow.

Finishing

PAINTING
Since wire sculpture is composed mostly of space, the lines must show up sharply against the background if they are to be seen properly. Painting in more than one colour has to be done very carefully, or parts of the work may not show up at all. Black, white, gold, silver, copper and the metallic colours all give a pleasing finish. You can use household paints or the small cans of enamel sold for model making, applied with a small artist's brush, but it is a laborious process as the painting must be done thinly and evenly, and two coats will be necessary.

Painting can be speeded up by using aerosol spray paints, which are sold in many colours and will put an even coat of paint on the wire. This is best done out of doors, and the spray must be moved continuously to cover every side of the wire.

PLASTIC COATING
A powdered plastic is available in the U.K. in various colours for coating wire. It can only be used over silver soldered joints as the temperature at which it melts is higher than that of soft solder. For really good results, special equipment is needed for melting the plastic onto the wire, so this method may be of more interest to groups or schools than to individual craftsmen.

6 Working in three dimensions

Fig 37   Tortoise

When you have mastered the design and construction of flat objects and become familiar with the technique of soldering and bending, you can begin to design and work in three dimensions. This presents quite a few problems, and ingenuity is needed to keep the various planes and forms of the sculpture understandable when viewed from any direction. In wood or stone carving the best side can be displayed but in wire sculpture nothing is hidden, even the inside becomes part of the design.

If we take a bird, for example, and try to represent every side of it in extreme detail, the result is likely to have the appearance of an unplanned bundle of wire and little of it will be clearly understood. It becomes quite a challenge to create a wire object which is effective from whichever angle it is seen. Wire sculpture needs a very light touch and an economical use of lines – the least indication possible to explain your ideas.

There are several ways to approach this problem of giving a solid but intelligible appearance to an object composed mainly of space. The first is to treat it as relief work, raised but designed

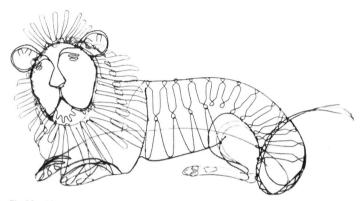

Fig 38   Lion

to be seen from only one direction, with no detail put into the back or underside. This type of sculpture needs to be displayed against a clear background, rather than in the centre of a room where it might be seen from the wrong viewpoint.

The tortoise illustrated in fig 37 has no underside and so has to be presented on a plain surface, but it gives the impression of being a complete sculpture.

Rather more complicated, but still avoiding trouble with the far side, the lion above is shaped as a complete sculpture in the round but is designed to lie on a surface and be seen from the front. Nothing lies behind the face, and the economical sketch of his superior expression shows the sort of thing that can be done in wire which is not possible in any other sculptural material. The continuous pattern following the line of the body gives a feeling both of rather loose supple skin and of a lithe animal ready for action.

A very useful idea in making a completely three-dimensional wire object is to use simple semi-flat sections set in different planes.

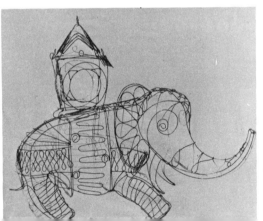

Fig 40   Elephant

Fig 39   Peacock

Thus the peacock in fig. 39, which is 32 in. long and seems quite advanced and difficult to make, is really a collection of fairly simple parts set at different angles. The over-all design of sweeping lines gives it an attractive quality. The almost flat tail has a strong framework, as it is long and unsupported. Each wing is absolutely flat. The body is only partially filled in, just enough to show its exact shape and position.

Even the feet are in quite different positions and again cannot puzzle the onlooker. All kinds of subjects can be used for sculptures made on this principle.

The elephant in fig. 40 is an example of the complete wire sculpture. The two sides of his body are identical, and made up of clearly defined parts, helping to lead the eye round his form. Since the ears are a very important feature, the spaces behind them are left unfilled. Similarly, the face has very little to complicate it.

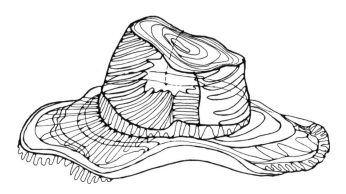

Fig 41   The old hat

As you try these methods of three-dimensional work, you should acquire the habit of standing back to study your unfinished sculpture from every angle and at every stage, attempting to picture the next step. This is even more necessary when a complete, free-standing piece is attempted. The details that are left out are almost as significant as the lines that are put in, and it is as well to stand each section of the sculpture in place and consider it carefully before actually putting it together. Be prepared to change your ideas and abandon anything that does not entirely satisfy you. It is certainly wise to draw a design on paper, but to keep too rigidly to the original idea can bring failure, as it is very hard to know just how the different parts are going to look when seen superimposed on one another.

These principles for making three-dimensional sculptures apply to any subject translated into wire, although it is easiest to demonstrate them on birds and animals. Figures particularly need careful thought and planning. Abstract sculpture and mobiles should either follow the rules suggested, or use can be made of the interplay of carefully organized lines which create changing patterns from each new point of view. For further ideas, see chapters 7 and 8.

The effective display of wire work needs careful consideration, and however well thought out the sculpture, it can become almost invisible against a muddled background or one which does not contrast sufficiently with the finished piece. Lighting is an important factor, and if side glints can be caught the three dimensions are better explained.

53

7 Ideas

With your equipment spread out in front of you and the urge to create giving you a feeling of excitement, it is disappointing when your imagination refuses to function and you wait fruitlessly for inspiration. Ideas are certainly elusive, but they are always synthesized from images gathered consciously or unconsciously in the mind, and it is wise to collect and record as many of these mind pictures and relevant facts as you can, to be built up afterwards into ideas.

Drawings

If you are collecting ideas for wire sculpture you should try to see in terms of line and space. One of the most helpful sources is the study of drawings. Every example of skilled draughtsmanship, ranging from today's newspaper cartoons back to ancient Chinese brushwork, shows an individual way of using lines, and each has something of interest to teach the wire sculptor. Notice the way lines are thickened for emphasis, the textures, the lines of

Fig 43   From a Mexican manuscript. British Museum

Fig 44   16th-century woodcut. British Museum

movement, the way artists economize and simplify while still fully expressing their ideas.

Old Egyptian paintings can give us lessons in repetition, while Persian drawings have an amusingly ornamental layout. Peasant embroidery and ceramic decoration which have become stylized by endless copying are full of charm and provide a rich store of ideas.

Fig 45   Ironwork

Fig 46   Wrought iron patterns

Patterns

In order to convey textures or fill spaces by purely decorative means, the lines must be organized into some kind of pattern, not necessarily regular. There are endless examples of linework from every country and every age, some of them unexpectedly modern. Ideas can be gleaned from old manuscripts where the penwork has run away into embellishments, in tooled leather, brass rubbings, old cane furniture, and wrought iron.

Doodles

Everyone likes doodling, so doodle with a purpose, or at least look at the results with wire sculpture in mind. From amongst many lines perhaps you will see an attractive shape which can be incorporated into the work. Above all if you are working with wire, then doodle with wire, and new ideas will emerge.

If you are on the alert for new ideas they will come from all sorts of unexpected directions.

Nature

Natural shapes and their variations, the interplay of one shape with another and the diversity of structure and surface, provide a vast field for inspiration. Look for the less usual, for patterns made by collections of natural objects, take one subject and try to depict it in all sorts of different ways.

The markings on a leaf or any other detail can be a starting point for a design which may finally have very little to show of the origins of the idea. Study the way plants and trees grow and the easy way the lines join, giving a feeling of harmony where awkward angles would be discordant.

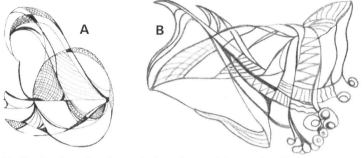

Fig 47   Doodles. **a** found on a telephone directory **b** from a school book

Fig 48
Natural lines

Fig 49   Patterns made by pylons

Fig 50 (*opposite*)   *Rainer's Chair*, 1965, by Harry Kramer. Albert Loeb and
        Krugier Gallery, New York. Iron wire and motors. A three-dimensional
        sculpture which does not look confused from any angle. Kramer has used
        wire as his medium for representing imaginary motion – opening up a new
        dimension in wire sculpture.

Ironwork and buildings

Having gained from the ideas of other artists and from nature, it
is time to look about for ideas from your own observations. Anything composed of lines set in more than one plane will offer a
changing patchwork of pieces as your viewpoint alters. The great
iron constructions from the last century have left us with a grand
store of bridges and ironwork which can be an inspiration for
sculpture, and modern scaffolding, pylons, oilrigs, cranes, ropes
and rigging give chance criss-crossing and grouping of lines
which would be difficult to invent.

   Architecture can present ideas for a composition of planes as
well as lines; look at clusters of modern buildings, old roofs, even
the pattern of shadows and buildings together.

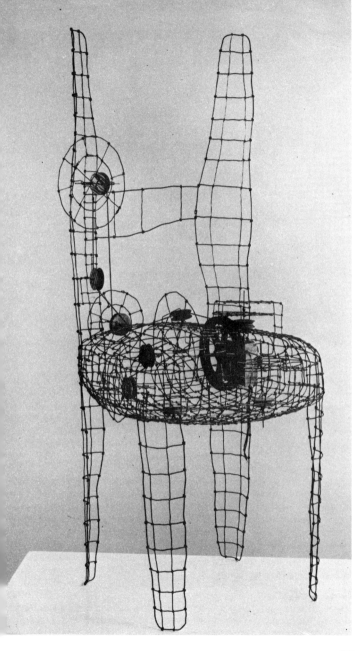

59

8 Birds and animals

Fig 51 Stork and giraffe

Many people who pick up a piece of wire for the first time
will form it into the outline of an animal or bird. This is partly
because of the practical and emotional ties we have with animals,
and partly because living forms provide us with such a tremendous
choice of models. The straightforward reporting on animal shapes
leads on to more elaborate sculptures, with textures and character,
and this is a good step towards figures and abstracts.

A wire animal, or any other subject for that matter, will not
come to life unless you have a sympathy for it, so choose a
creature that really interests you, that seems to you to be an
individual – possibly a pet at home, or some animal you see
frequently and know well. Then you will be seeing it as a particular shape in space and as a definite character which has to be
brought out in the way you use the wire.

Where to start

Since wire sculpture is composed only of lines, the solid body and
its personality must be translated into lines. Drawing helps to tidy
up the ideas in your head, so use a thick pencil or felt pen for
quick drawings of the whole design and of individual details.

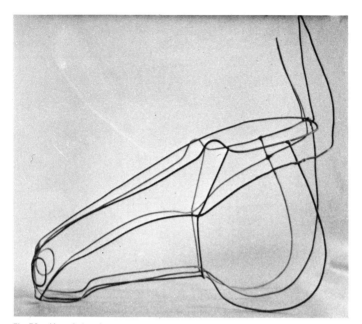

Fig 52 Horse's head

Following a very carefully planned and drawn design can be restricting as it does not allow you to alter or develop an idea as you begin to see the wire turning into a sculpture. However, you should consider at each stage how to minimize the number of joints, and it can be helpful to sketch quickly some thoughts on each section as you come to it.

Ideas for animal sculptures can start from such different sources that it is not possible to give a set pattern of procedure. If it is the outline that you want to emphasize, make this first and complete the sculpture in such a way that the general lines and position continue to be the most important feature. The stork in fig. 51 has a decorative curve of head and body and is treated very simply, so that the contours are not confused with detail.

Or perhaps an amusing expression takes your fancy; capture this first and build up your design around it. Once a creature has an expression it seems to be alive and the following stages come more easily. The lion in fig. 38 is an example of a sculpture which grew from the facial expression into a complete animal.

Markings, scales or shell patterns can also spark off the desire to make a sculpture. The giraffe in fig. 51 began like this and grew out of the attempt to represent his patchwork markings.

Fig 53 Cat

To make a piece interesting, avoid setting the head and body perfectly straight. Turn the head sideways, looking up or down, curve the body, have one leg forward, keep every part lively. It is, however, possible to overdo the liveliness, so try not to allow movement to become contortion.

The feeling of the weight of a strong animal, the grace of a bird or the creepiness of a spider are all important aspects of each character, and should be considered in the conception of a design. Let the lines of a heavy creature follow the muscle of the shoulders, all the lines of weight being directed downwards, with the texture heavy and adding to the feeling of solidity. For a light, elegant bird use sweeping horizontal lines and let them flow into one another, with the representation of texture also in a graceful style to give the feeling of buoyancy (see fig. 70). Every part of the composition should have some bearing on what you are trying to convey.

Details

The general lines and movement of a sculpture are first seen as a

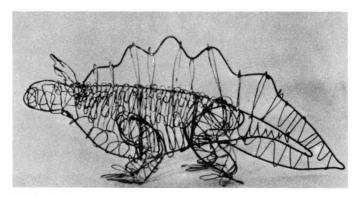

Fig 54   Reptile

whole, but every good sculpture should be worth looking at more carefully. There ought to be more to discover and to please as you move closer.

Give careful thought to every part, so that each individual section is well designed and also adds to the over-all look of the sculpture. It is good training in observation and interpretation to try various ways of indicating a particular natural texture, using either a naturalistic style or a freer, more abstract pattern.

Fig 55   Spider

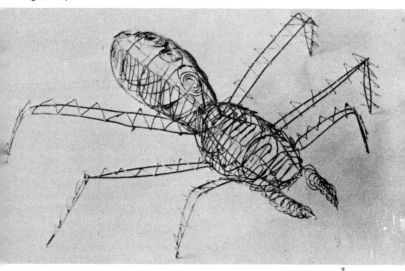

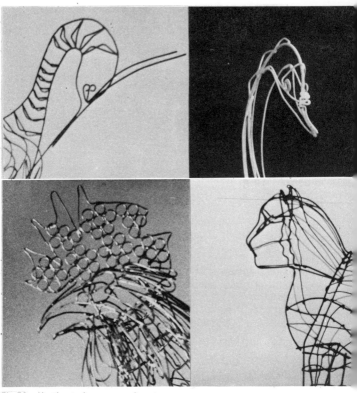

Fig 56   Heads: stork, swan, cock, cat

In animal and bird subjects the head and features help to
establish the personality, but to make them intelligible the lines
need to be simplified as much as possible without losing the
main points of difference between one creature and another. With
the lightest touch, expressions of, say, ferocity, haughtiness or
mildness can be shown, and the details are easily supplied by the
imagination of the spectator. Insects and fish can have definite
faces or not, depending on the style of your work. Fig. 56 shows
the heads of several sculptures, treated in a variety of ways.

Feet and legs too are very expressive and even when made in

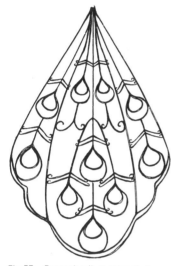

Fig 57   Peacock tail, tortoise shell

the plainest way can still convey whether they are dainty or hefty, wrinkled or elegant.

Tails, wings, fins, shells, spines and markings can all be themes for exciting experiments in wire work; every part should be a vital clue to the whole.

In fig. 57 you will see that the peacock tail is done in a naturalistic way, using the shape of the feathers to build up the design, while the tortoise shell, although not entirely unlike the real thing, has as many variations as possible to make an interesting and decorative texture.

Fig 58   Parts of stylized cat shown in fig. 59

Stylized animals

A lot of fun can be found in making stylized animals, still recognizable but with the accent on design and decoration. The cat in fig. 59 is amusing and very simple to make, being only slightly rounded and about 8 in. high. Using 16g galvanized wire, it can be glued or soldered as most of the parts are prefabricated. Fig. 58 shows the separate parts. After making the body frame, individual ways of filling-in can be invented, but keep the bends smooth and even; kinks and irregular spacing give a generally untidy effect although each separate fault may not be noticeable. The outline of the head and ears is made from one length of wire with the ends soldered together, and is curved a little so that it is not completely flat. Assemble all the small pieces of the features flat and solder them together, leaving long enough whiskers to attach the section to the head frame. The head and body are joined at two points, and finally the tail, made from a long wire wound round a pencil, is added to complete the piece.

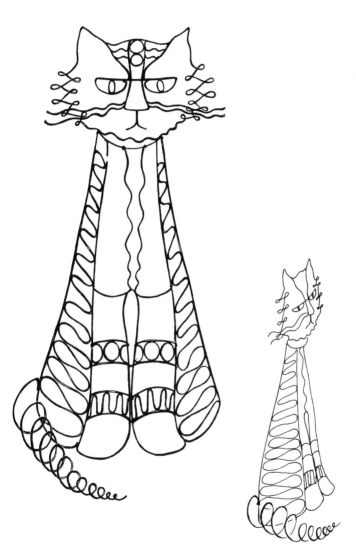

Fig 59   Stylized cat

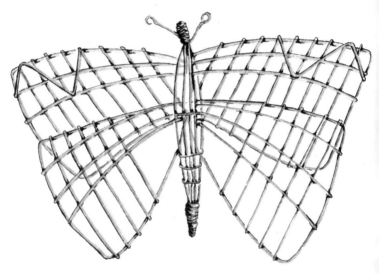

Fig 60   Butterfly

Fig 61 (*opposite*)   Baby owl. Several new ideas, using a spring as body outline, eyes wound with cotton, metal spirals from turning

Subjects

Instead of confining your work to single birds, animals or insects in their natural state, you could go further afield and look for subjects among animals in use, in action or in groups: caparisoned horses, circus animals, Spanish fighting bulls, dressed elephants, a shoal of fish; or heraldic and mythological beasts: griffon, phoenix or dragon.

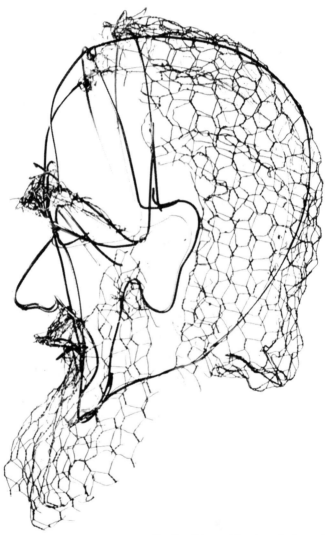

Fig 62   Old man. 10g wire and wire netting

9 Figures and abstracts

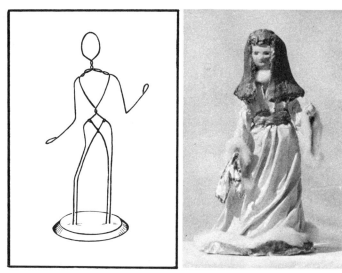

Fig 63   Armature and plaster figure made by a 12-year-old

Figures

Since much human emotion is conveyed by gestures and the
position of the body, wire can be used to create interesting figure
sculptures, picking out the important lines of movement and
expression. Groups of figures must be carefully organized and all
unnecessary lines abandoned, an excellent training in reaching
the heart of the theme and keeping detail to its proper level of
importance.

WIRE FRAMES AND ARMATURES

Plaster and clay models must be built on a sturdy wire armature;
this is just a soldered core of 12g–16g galvanized wire (depending
on the size of the figure) set in a plaster or wood base. When the
relative length of each part of the figure is right, and the relationship of the parts to one another is well observed, there will be no

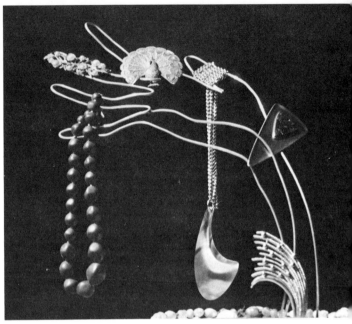

Fig 64   Wire work for shop window display

difficulty in building up a correctly proportioned figure. If the
original wire armature is inaccurate then it is impossible to
produce a good finished sculpture. The variations in child and
adult forms should be studied and also the way the body
compensates for one movement by another to keep it in balance.

For frames which are to be covered in fabric, a more complete
structure is needed, with the head and body modelled in wire.
These are padded, and dressed in suitable material for ornamental
dolls and puppets.

Figures and parts of figures in wire make unusual stands for
window dressing and exhibitions. In an unconfused setting they
provide a very eye-catching display.

FIGURES IN SCULPTURE
Flat wire figures in all kinds of styles offer a great variety of ideas
for pictures, table tops under glass or hanging decorations. For
instance, formalized figures in white wire on a black background
panel have the feeling of a brass rubbing. Or a group of people
treated in a contemporary style would suit a modern room.

Fig 65   Flat wire figure in
the style of a brass rubbing

Fig 66   Nativity scene. Three-dimensional figures approx. 18 in. high, made of 16g galvanized wire painted white, and displayed against a dark background in Salisbury Cathedral at Christmas

Three-dimensional groups or single forms have to be well displayed, and the suggestions in chapter 6 for organizing three-dimensional sculptures must be kept in mind so that they remain understandable and full of character.

The more you use wire to interpret figures, the more fascinating the study becomes, especially if you extend your range of materials to include wire netting, barbed wire, or cotton and string (see frontispiece and page 69) where these will genuinely add to the meaning of the sculpture. The use of wire netting in the old man (fig. 62, page 70) adds to the feeling of age and is an indispensable part of the work.

Fig 67   Refugees. 8 in. high, 18g galvanized wire. Three-dimensional but with no back. This type of semi-three-dimensional sculpture stands easily on a narrow shelf or can be hung against a wall.

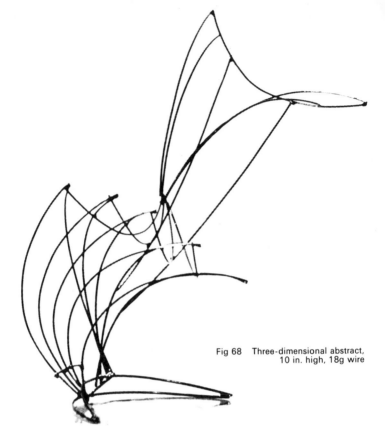

Fig 68 Three-dimensional abstract,
10 in. high, 18g wire

Abstracts

Natural forms make a good starting point for wire sculpture as it is easier to view your own work critically when using familiar shapes and proportions. But as soon as you use wire to interpret a solid object you are already studying abstract design, the relationship between line and space, and the effects of lines superimposed on each other. You have used abstract patterns to represent texture, and thought about weight and movement in terms of lines. So it is not a very big step to work entirely in abstract terms.

PANELS

Carrying on from the simple wall-decorations mentioned on pages 45 and 46, build up more elaborate panels using several sizes of wire. Divide the space into irregular rectangles and fill

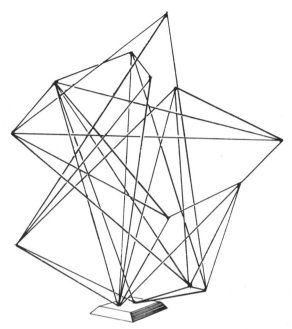

Fig 69   Three-dimensional abstract using straight wires

each one with a different texture to contrast with its neighbours, and stand back as you work to see the effect from a distance. As well as an interesting decoration, you will have a reference library of ideas always on view.

THREE-DIMENSIONAL ABSTRACTS
To make three-dimensional sculptures, it is best at first to limit yourself in some way. Take straight wires of the same length and two different gauges and build these up into an architectural abstract. Remember to keep turning the work round so that the design is balanced. Or use equal pieces cut from a roll of wire, with the curve unaltered, to construct a sculpture.

Fig. 69 shows an abstract made up of lengths of straight wire. Various arrangements were tried out by pushing the wires into a lump of clay until a satisfying combination of lines gave a start to the sculpture.

Norbert Kricke's sculpture in fig. 42 (page 53) shows the use of straight rods built up to create a sculpture of great feeling. Although this is welded, the same sort of design could be made with lengths of straight wire soldered together.

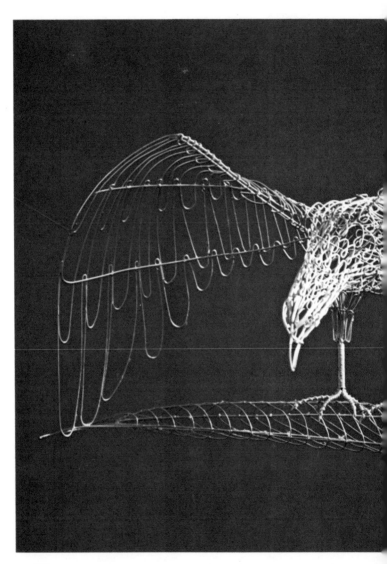

Fig 70 Osprey. 2 ft. 6 in. wide, 16g galvanized wire, painted. A very carefully organized and strongly constructed three-dimensional wire sculpture

Fig 71   Two views of a partly finished abstract

Fig 72 (*opposite*)   Finished abstract

Another method of creating a complex but unconfused abstract, is to bend a number of similar units of wire to the same shape, and make the fullest use of different angles and combinations in building them up.

An entirely different type of abstract sculpture is possible by taking a single thick brass wire and sweeping it into an open knot; consider it from every side until you are satisfied that the curves are absolutely smooth and the design is right from any angle. Thicken it with extra wires for emphasis, without destroying the clean curve, or wind thin wire between some parts to show the planes.

Starting with this idea of a simple knot, a sculpture can be built up to any degree of complexity. The completed abstract shown in fig. 72 and on the cover, was begun with a single twist, using 16g and 18g galvanized wire, and elaborated gradually without any pre-planning. The two views in fig. 71, of the same sculpture before completion, illustrate the change of shape in a three-dimensional design as the viewpoint alters.

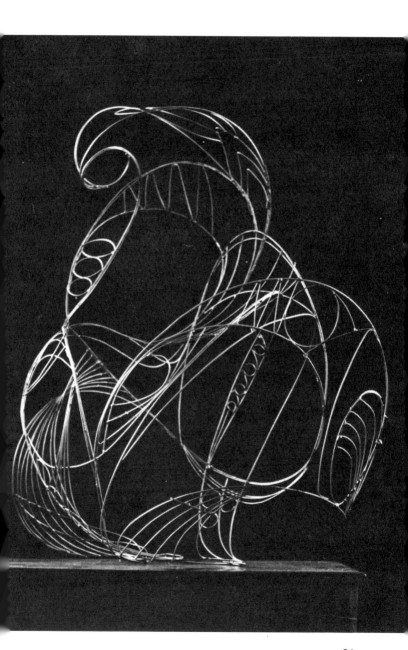

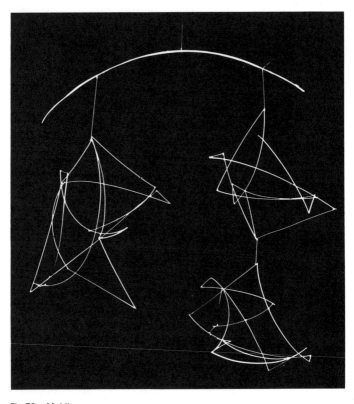

Fig 73 Mobile

Mobiles

Hanging from the ceiling and moving in the air currents or resting on pivots on the ground, mobiles are studies in balance, both in actual weight – they must hang evenly – and in visual weight. Some contrast in the size of the separate parts is necessary but the whole effect should be that of equilibrium.

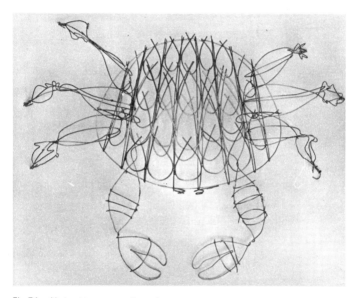

Fig 74   Abstract treatment of a crab

Mobiles are usually abstract shapes, but you can have plenty of fun experimenting with different subjects; try mobiles to decorate a room for a particular occasion, or mobiles with a Christmas flavour.

10   Wire work in the home

Fig 75   Swan

Wire craft, either naturalistic or abstract, is an attractive addition
to the interior decoration of the home. It combines the lightness
and cheerfulness of a bowl of flowers with the permanence and
artistic feeling of solid sculpture. Many difficult corners and bare
walls can be transformed by individual wire sculptures, designed
to suit the style of the room. But apart from pure decoration, wire
can be put to useful purposes about the house.

Here are a few suggestions, and I am sure you will find many
more ideas to suit your own home.

Plant and flower holders

A simple plant support was shown in chapter 5 and more complicated climbing frames could be made for very energetic plants;
they should be pleasant to look at even before the plant is fully
grown.

Cut flowers can be arranged in front of, or through, almost any
wire structure, and a constant change of decoration is obtained
in this way. The swan shown here sits over a small vase and the
flowers are supported by the back and wings (see also fig. 12).

Plant pot holders to hang on the wall, or a cover to disguise an

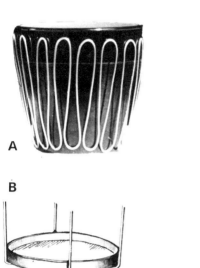

A

B

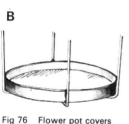

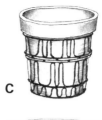

C

D

Fig 76　Flower pot covers

unattractive pot, are useful outlets for wire work. Since the back of the work is hidden, you can employ very close and intricate patterns. Fig. 76a shows the simplest design, which is made in brass wire and stretches to fit most pots; c and d are more elaborate. The wire can be soldered onto a suitable metal lid for a complete pot holder (b), or if the wires are carried across the bottom a dish can be dropped into the base.

Coffee table

A brass wire design sandwiched between a coloured board and a sheet of glass makes a very smart table top. Using a plastic-coated board in a plain strong colour, arrange on it a design in 12g brass wire – it could be abstract, pictorial or formal. The cleaned and lacquered pieces of wire must be shaped exactly and should lie flat with no crossing over. Glue these to the board very cleanly with impact glue. Lay a sheet of thick glass over this, and edge it with strips of wood, picture framing or plastic edging; the glass must be held down very firmly over the wire. Use a set of screw-on legs to complete the table.

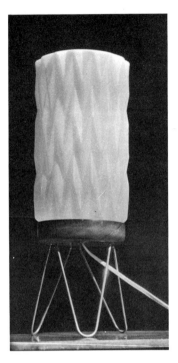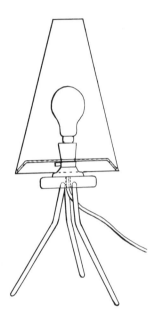

Fig 77   Lamps

Lamps

Use 10g brass wire to make legs for simple contemporary lamp bases. The style of legs and the type of lampshade to be used should be part of the over-all design, but the basis is a disc of polished wood, with a hole in the centre for the electric wire. The brass legs are either threaded through holes bored to a tight fit, or pushed into incomplete holes on the underside of the disc and glued in place with resin glue. A suitable lamp-fitting is screwed onto the wood and wired up.

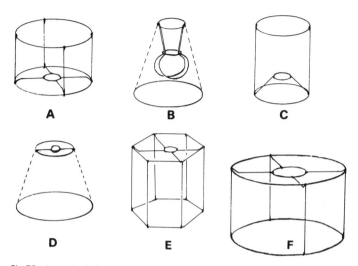

Fig 78   Lampshade frames.
a, b, c for table lamps d, e for hanging lights f standard lamp – the centre
fitting varies with different lamps

Lampshade frames

With the wide choice of parchment and lampshade covering
now available, it is useful to be able to make frames of just the
right shape and size to suit a lamp you have made or to modernize a
light you already have at home.

Use 16g galvanized wire, and if the shade is to be screwed onto
the fitting, shape the centre carefully to fit snugly under the
screw ring. For a shade which sits on the bulb make sure the grip
is tight enough to keep the shade in place but does not require too
much force to push it onto the bulb. See that the shade itself is
held well away from the heat with a good-sized ventilation hole
at the top. If possible use silver solder for strength.

Stiff parchment does not generally need wires joining the top
and bottom rings of the frame, and the appearance of the lamp
when lit is better without them.

For ideas of different shapes of frames and covering, look at
commercial lamps, Chinese lantern styles and frames designed
for home lampshade making.

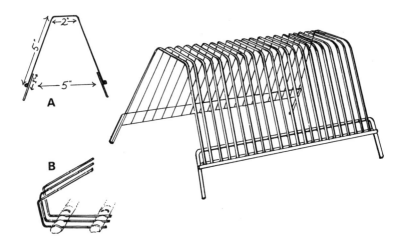

Fig 79   Record rack

Record rack

A rack for 7 in. records is shown in fig. 79. The best results
are obtained by using straight wire, as it is essential to get the
spacing accurate and this is not easy with rolled wire which is
inclined to twist out of place.

Cut 12 in. lengths of 12g or 14g straight galvanized wire for as
many partitions as you want – don't be too ambitious – and bend
them as shown (a). Lay out two long, even 'sausages' of
plasticine or clay on the bench, marking them both as precisely
as possible to leave $\frac{1}{8}$ in. between each section. Press the wires
into these marks (b), if necessary arranging a support for the
side above. Lay the cross piece and leg over these wires, and
solder at each point. Turn the whole rack over carefully and solder
the other leg and cross wire. Finish by soldering an outer cross wire
to tidy the appearance of the cut ends. If you have facilities
for plastic coating, use silver solder and coat in coloured plastic
to give a nicely finished article.

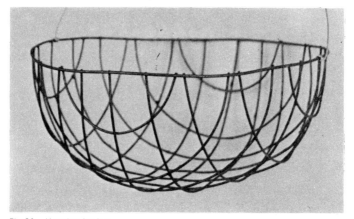

Fig 80   Hanging basket

Garden

Wire is always useful in the garden for ties, hoops for the tall plants, or wires for training climbers against the house.

HANGING BASKETS FOR TRAILING PLANTS

A straightforward heavy mesh basket is shown in fig. 80, using 10g wire to give enough strength to hold its shape when filled with plants. Design the basket according to the position it will occupy: this simple type for hanging at a distance, or a more interesting pattern for a front porch or wall.

WILD BIRD FEEDER

Deep narrow food containers for the smaller birds are often made of wire netting, but pleasanter wire baskets with lids look pretty hanging on the bird table.

Fig 81   Small bird feeder

Fig 82 (*opposite*)   Christmas card holder

Fig 83   Christmas decoration

Christmas decorations

With dazzling silver and gold paint to catch the lights, Christmas decorations are an excuse for quickly made, gay and not necessarily lasting bits and pieces: little stars, balls, snow crystals hung on strings to move and sparkle; or bigger mobiles, Christmas card stands and table decorations.

CHRISTMAS TREE

Take strips of 18g wire from 4 to 12 in. long, curl each end inside the natural curve, and bend back at the middle using narrow pliers to give a sharp angle. Double over a 24 in. length of wire, twist lightly two thirds of the way down and open out the base for the trunk. Grade the branches in size and solder down the stem with two small branches below the largest one (fig. 83).

To make a standing tree, slip similar branches at right angles through the flat tree, attaching with glue to avoid unsoldering the first joints.

CARD HOLDER

Christmas cards are difficult to arrange in the house; one solution is to make a wire stand with a seasonal flavour, leaving free ends in the design to hold the cards (fig. 82).

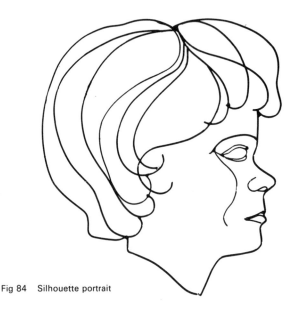

Fig 84   Silhouette portrait

There are many possible uses for wire craft at home; only a few are demonstrated here. Every household has different needs and every craftsman produces different inventions and ideas. It is hoped that this book will set you on the way to finding out and creating for yourself.

Here are just two more ideas which you might like to enlarge upon.

WINE BOTTLE BASKET
To hold a bottle for easy pouring. A chance for decorative and inventive wire work which would look well on the dinner table.

PORTRAITS
If you are good at likenesses with simple pencil lines, why not try a two-dimensional portrait in wire, a type of silhouette, of a member of your family?

11 Making things for children

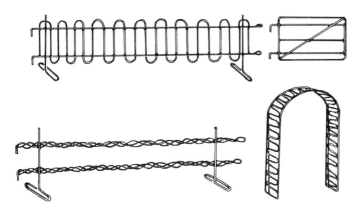

Fig 85   Fences and gates for model farms

The ability to work and solder wire is infinitely useful in toy making. Of course, for the very young child wire can be dangerous to play with; but for older children there is a wealth of small-scale work to be done. It is good discipline to make toys, as the constant handling will quickly show up poor construction.

Care should be taken not to leave sharp ends of wire unprotected.

Farm and zoo

Every young owner of a model farm or zoo is in constant need of fences, gates and cages and these can be quickly made with 18g or 20g wire. If you are repeating a lot of pieces you can arrange a suitable jig, but for a few sections or an interesting variety of designs it is better to do them unaided.

FENCES AND GATES

Make two uprights with sturdy feet for each section of fence, and solder these to two cross wires with a hook on one end and a loop in the other (fig. 85). Solder onto this any continuous design, plaited (braided) wire or straight pieces, to make sectional fences which are easily hooked together for any shape of field.

Gates can be made to fit into the fence system, using hooks as hinges to fit the fence loops.

Fig 86   Cage section, aviary and round enclosure for model zoos

CAGES

Zoo cages are simple to construct, either on the same principle as the fencing with continuous wire bending, or by using a series of similar shapes soldered onto cross wires. For the giraffe's cage in fig. 86 the 4 in. lengths of straight wire are curved over at the top, laid on a roll of clay so that the spacing and set of the pieces are kept even, and soldered onto the cross bars. Tall sections need wide feet to keep them upright.

The aviary is made from hoops arranged in a circle. Stand them in clay to get the spacing right, solder the top where all the hoops cross, and fit rings of wire over the aviary at intervals to hold the wires in place, soldering wherever possible. Trim the bottom if necessary and wash off the clay before fixing the final ring. If the base is cut from sandpaper and a wooden perch added the result is quite realistic.

Round cheese boxes with continuously bent wire edging make simple and quickly constructed enclosures.

94

Fig 87   Hanging wall decoration for children. 16g galvanized wire, soldered

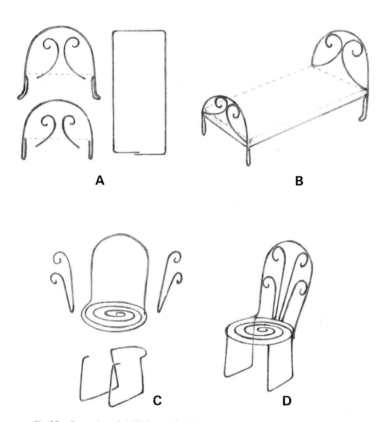

Fig 88   Examples of doll's house furniture.
          a pieces of bed **b** finished bed **c** pieces of chair **d** finished chair

Dolls' house

The manufacture of miniature furniture, made with 18g or 20g wire, gives scope for fascinating designs in beds and chairs; legs and frames for tables or for upholstered chairs; lamps and small accessories. The work is delicate and needs to be very neatly soldered or glued.

For a home-made dolls' house, wire work can be employed in leaded window panes, balconies, stair banisters or a spiral staircase, and perhaps for a trellis on the outer walls and a wrought iron and glass front door.

Fig 89   Small wire ornaments, 2–3 in. high

Model railways and roads

For adding to a railway set, or making a model road system more exciting, use wire for fences, level crossing gates, girder bridges, frames for tunnels or hill climbs, and for signals and road signs.

Small creatures and figures

Children like small-scale ornaments and appreciate the humour of these drawings in space. Use thin wire and try to give them plenty of character; they can be flat or three-dimensional.

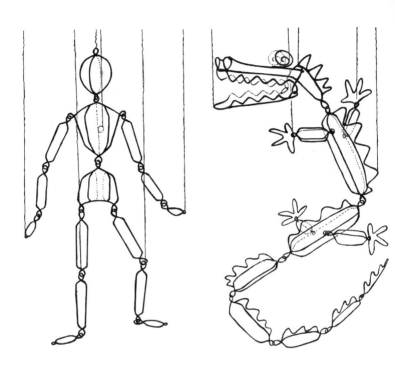

Fig 90   Puppet frames

Puppets

Loosely linked wire units, with provision for attaching the strings, make a basis for very free moving puppets to be clothed in various ways. The heads can be covered in material or papier mâché. It may be found easier to control these very light puppets if the feet are weighted with plasticine, or with lead wrappers from wine-bottle corks melted down and formed into a suitable shape.

This method of puppet-making is easily adapted to creating all sorts and shapes of animal puppets.

Fig 91   Crown

Dressing up

Children love to have an array of dressing-up clothes at home, and school plays often call for head-dresses and wings which are not always easy to make successfully. Wire frames with a paper or fabric covering can be adapted to many needs.

TIARAS
Constructed of fine wire in delicate designs and painted in gold or silver.

CROWNS
Gold-painted wire, enriched with velvet and glass beads, or more simply with coloured paper (fig. 91).

HELMETS, SHIELDS AND ARMOUR
These can all be built up on a wire frame (fig. 92).

WINGS
Make a frame in 16g wire, with provision for tying on tapes or pinning to a dress, and cover in tissue paper or muslin (fig. 93).

ANIMAL HEADS
These should be made as light as possible with the frame fitting over the shoulders to keep the head in place; cover in very light fabric or paper.

Note When making articles for children to wear it is particularly important to double over all sharp ends and bind them with tape to avoid any chance of scratches.

Fig 92   Knight's helmet. Wire frame to fit over a riding hat, covered with painted cardboard and silver foil

Fig 93   Wings.
   a covered in tissue paper **b** simple frame

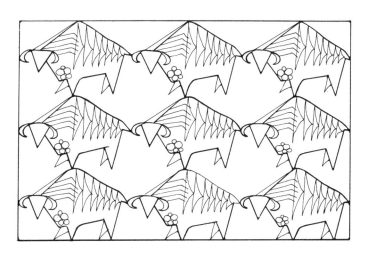

Conclusion

Wire is a good material for sculpture and the results are very satisfying, but because it can only be applied to relatively small and carefully displayed work you may feel the need to add some solid materials. Pieces cut from old tin cans, springs, washers, metal gauze and all kinds of light oddments from the scrap heap can be incorporated with the wire, using solder or glue. For larger work with heavy metal, solder is not strong enough; brazing or welding is essential.

However large and ingenious your constructions become, the study of wire sculpture will give your work a lightness of touch and freshness of approach which will help to make them both distinctive and exciting.

Fig 96   War horse. Welded metal, including springs, washers, old file blade, metal gauze, meat skewers

List of suppliers

AUTOMATIC SPIRIT (ALCOHOL) BLOWPIPE
Valtock Ltd, Warwick Street, London W1 and from hardware stores

EPOXY RESIN GLUE (ARALDITE AY111)
CIBA (ARL) Ltd, Duxford. Cambridge and from hardware stores

GAS TORCH
Sievert, Sweden and from hardware stores

PLASTIC COATING POWDER (TELCOTHENE LD)
Telcon Plastics Ltd, Green Street Green, Orpington, Kent

SOLDER AND FLUX
Fry's Metals Ltd, Tandem Works, Merton Abbey, London SW19

BAKER'S SOLDERING FLUXES
Sir Wm Burnett & Co., and from hardware stores

LOW TEMPERATURE BRAZING ALLOYS AND FLUX
Johnson Matthey Metals Ltd, 81 Hatton Garden, London EC1

WIRE:
silver Johnson Matthey Metals Ltd, address as above
brass and copper J. Smith and Sons, Senier-Stanton Division, 49 St John's Square, London EC1
galvanized from hardware stores

ADHESIVES FOR BONDING
Hardware stores

BLOWPIPES AND TORCHES
Hardware and department stores

SOLDERING EQUIPMENT
from hardware stores, welding and metalworking suppliers

WIRE:
silver T. B. Hagstoz & Co., 707 Sansom St, Philadelphia, Pennsylvania
brass and copper from hardware stores and builders' suppliers

Index